WILDFIRE
INSIDE THE INFERNO

by Jaclyn Jaycox

CAPSTONE PRESS
a capstone imprint

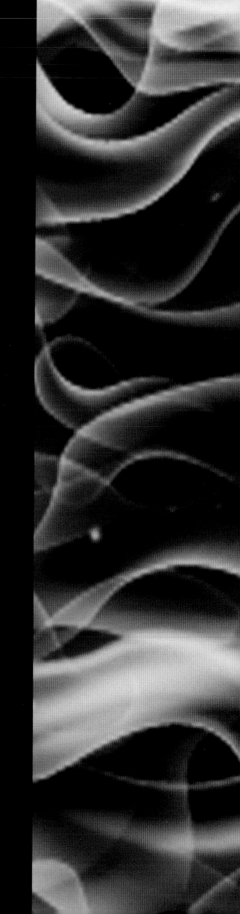

Published by Capstone Press, an imprint of Capstone
1710 Roe Crest Drive, North Mankato, Minnesota 56003
capstonepub.com

Library of Congress Cataloging-in-Publication Data
Names: Jaycox, Jaclyn, 1983- author.
Title: Wildfire, inside the inferno / by Jaclyn Jaycox.
Description: North Mankato, Minnesota : Capstone Press, an imprint of Capstone, [2023] | Includes bibliographical references and index. | Audience: Ages 8-11 | Audience: Grades 4-6 | Summary: "Wildfires rip through forests, choke the air with smoke, and destroy homes. Some wildfires are sparked by nature. Others are started by humans. All come with devastating results. Readers will find out the science behind wildfires, learn about recent wildfires around the world, and discover what's being done to prevent them. Dynamic photography and clear, engaging text will captivate the reader's attention"—Provided by publisher.
Identifiers: LCCN 2022022217 (print) | LCCN 2022022218 (ebook) | ISBN 9781684466115 (hardcover) | ISBN 9781669036272 (paperback) | ISBN 9781684466078 (pdf) | ISBN 9781684466092 (kindle edition)
Subjects: LCSH: Wildfires—Juvenile literature.
Classification: LCC SD421.23 .J393 2023 (print) | LCC SD421.23 (ebook) | DDC 634.9/618—dc23/eng/20220607
LC record available at https://lccn.loc.gov/2022022217
LC ebook record available at https://lccn.loc.gov/2022022218

Editorial Credits
Editor: Erika L. Shores; Designer: Hilary Wacholz; Media Researcher: Jo Miller; Production Specialist: Tori Abraham

Image Credits
Alamy: Mint Images Limited, 27 (middle), Natural History Archive, 18 (bottom), NPS Photo, 29 (bottom); Associated Press: Noah Berger, 6, bottom, 7, 25; Getty Images: AFP/DIMITAR DILKOFF, 9 (top), Barbara Rich, 6 (top), Bettmann, 19, David McNew, 24, John Crux Photography, 14, SOPA Images, 5; Shutterstock: Ajax9, 26 (bottom), Austin Hawley, 26 (middle), Chris Ison, 16, Christian Roberts-Olsen, back cover, David A Litman, 22, Dima Aslanian, 10 (bottom), Fabien Monteil, 26 (top), GypsyPictureShow, 15 (top), Igor Bukhlin, 10 (top), Jaden Schaul, 21, 23, Jason Benz Bennee, 13, Lumppini, 11 (bottom), LuYago, 9 (bottom), My Photo Buddy, 18 (top), NPstock, 11 (top), petroleum man, 12 (top), Phillip Wittke, 27 (top), Photo Spirit, 17, Robert Wilder Jr, 28, Sergey Spritnyuk, 12 (bottom), stockpexel, cover, 1, Sunil P Nair, 11 (middle), TD wt, 29 (top), Trzmiel, 8, Urri, 27 (bottom), VectorMine, 15 (bottom), Ververidis Vasilis, 20

Design Elements:
Shutterstock: Olga Moonlight, Vectomart, WinWin artlab

All internet sites appearing in back matter were available and accurate when this book was sent to press.

Printed and bound in China. PO5130

CONTENTS

CHAPTER 1

A WORLD ON FIRE

The sky is gray and hazy. The smell of smoke fills the air. In the distance there's a roar, like a freight train. Flames rush through the forest, engulfing everything in their path. Lush green trees turn to blazing matchsticks. A wildfire has begun.

On July 13, 2021, a tree in the Feather River Canyon in California fell onto a power line. When a power company worker went to investigate, he found a fire near the base of the tree. At that point, the fire was estimated to be 40 feet by 40 feet (12 meters by 12 meters). That's about the size of a three-car garage.

Firefighters soon arrived and got to work. They used water from the river to try to drown the flames. But strong winds and rugged terrain made progress difficult. By late evening, the fire had grown to cover between one and five acres (0.4 and 2 hectares). But by the next morning, it had spread to more than 500 acres (200 ha). It was named the Dixie Fire, after a road near its starting point.

Smoke blocks out a highway as spreading flames engulf trees during the Dixie Fire.

The Dixie Fire continued to spread. Large wildfires can make their own weather. The blaze soon created enough heat to form a fire cloud. Fire clouds are just like thunderclouds. They bring strong winds. They spread the fire even faster in all directions. At least a dozen lightning strikes burst out of the clouds. They made

it dangerous for firefighters. The lightning also risked hitting trees and starting new fires. But one thing these clouds don't usually create is a lot of rain. So the fire raged on, quickly covering more ground.

FACT
The Dixie Fire was classified as a "megafire." Megafires burn at least 100,000 acres (40,469 hectares) of land and have a huge impact on people and the environment.

The Dixie Fire burned for more than three months. It tore through nearly 1 million acres (404,686 hectares). Thousands of people in the fire's path were evacuated. More than 1,300 buildings and homes were destroyed. The small town of Greenville was completely devastated. The aftermath looked like something out of a movie. Deserted streets could be seen through a thick cloud of smoke. Smoldering piles of debris and ash lay where buildings used to stand.

The destruction left behind by the Dixie Fire in Greenville, California

The Dixie Fire was the largest single wildfire in California's history. But it was not the worst fire in the world in 2021. While the Dixie Fire raged in the U.S., people in Russia were battling an even larger blaze.

SIBERIAN WILDFIRES

Siberia is in Russia. It is one of the coldest places on Earth, but for the past few years, the area has had very dry and hot weather. Wildfires began to break out there in June. They spread and grew at an alarming rate. At one point, more than 250 fires were burning across the region.

The smoke was so thick, people couldn't see more than a block away. Even people that weren't in the path of the fire were told to stay indoors. The air wasn't safe to breathe. Satellites picked up images of the smoke from space. The smoke reached areas thousands of miles away. It is the first time in recorded history smoke from a wildfire reportedly reached the North Pole.

A satellite image shows the widespread fires in Siberia in 2021.

An overhead view of a Siberian forest fire

By August, the wildfires in Russia were larger than the rest of the world's wildfires combined. It also became the biggest blaze in Russia's history. More than 45 million acres (18.1 million hectares) were burned. That is almost the size of the U.S. state of Washington. This was a record-breaking year around the globe for wildfires.

The view from the ground of a Siberian wildfire

CHAPTER 2

ALL ABOUT WILDFIRES

Wildfires are uncontrolled fires in nature. They happen all around the world. Wildfires have burned in North and South America, Europe, Australia, Asia, North Africa, and even in the Arctic. They are most likely to occur during the dry, warm months of the year. The less moisture, the easier it is for a fire to start.

Wildfires can start from a natural event, such as a lightning strike. Strong heat from the sun on dry grass and plants can also cause a fire. But most often, humans start them. Usually, it is by accident. Campfires have been left unattended. Burning ash floats away from the fire. Shooting off fireworks in a dry, wooded area can also cause a fire. Under the right conditions, even a small piece of burning debris from a campfire or fireworks can start a wildfire.

TYPES OF WILDFIRES

GROUND FIRES: They start below the surface. They begin when plant roots or other dry, dead materials under the soil ignite. Lightning often starts ground fires.

SURFACE FIRES: They happen above the surface. Dry plants and grasses on or near the ground burn.

CROWN FIRES: They burn through tree canopies. These fires can spread quickly. It is the area least protected from the wind.

There are only three ingredients needed to start a wildfire: heat, fuel, and oxygen. When they meet, it's a recipe for disaster.

Fuel can be anything flammable. Typically, the fuel for a wildfire is trees, grass, or leaves. The drier the fuel, the easier it will burn. These fuels give off gases called vapors. When the heat, such as a spark, comes in contact with the vapors, they ignite.

Oxygen is the final ingredient. A fire can't start or continue without it. Think of a burning candle in a jar. If you put the lid on the jar, the flame dies out. But when it comes to wildfires, it's impossible to take away all the oxygen.

Dry grasses in a field burn as wind spreads the flames.

THE UPSIDE

Wildfires may seem scary, but they can actually be helpful. Forests can get overgrown. Trees start competing for water. There isn't always enough water, so many trees will die. Too many trees and leaves can also block out sunlight from the forest floor. Plants can't grow without sunlight. Many forest animals rely on these plants for food. When a wildfire happens, it clears away the dead trees. New plants begin to grow. It's once again a good home for animals.

New grass grows among trees charred by fire.

Unfortunately, not all wildfires have a positive impact. In recent years, wildfires have become bigger and far more destructive. What is causing these massive infernos?

CHAPTER 3

ENVIRONMENTAL FACTORS

In June 2019, bushfires in Australia began to pop up. Hot temperatures, dry weather, and strong winds quickly worsened the situation. By September, the wildfires were out of control. It wasn't until March 2020 that the fires were put out or contained. They left behind complete devastation. More than 45 million acres (18 million hectares) of land had been scorched. Nearly 6,000 homes and buildings were destroyed. Thirty-four people were killed, including several firefighters who were battling the blazes. Australia has dealt with bushfires many times before. But this fire season was particularly bad.

Flames spread and smoke billows during Australia's 2019 bushfires.

CLIMATE CHANGE

There are a number of factors that help produce these incredible wildfires. One is climate change. Things people do every day help cause climate change. We use energy to drive cars and keep our houses warm or cool. Energy comes from burning oil, gas, and coal. When these things are burned, it puts gases into the air. These are known as greenhouse gases. They trap heat, making the air warm up. This can change the normal weather patterns and temperatures of places.

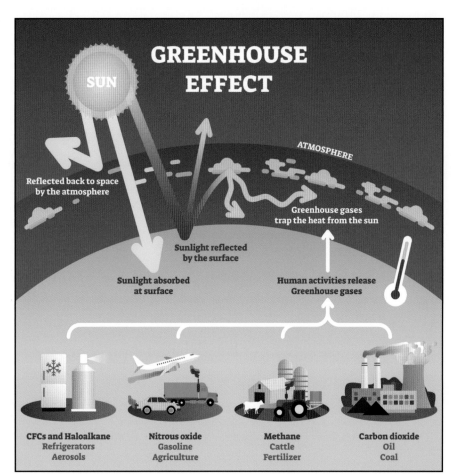

GREENHOUSE EFFECT

SUN

Reflected back to space by the atmosphere

ATMOSPHERE

Greenhouse gases trap the heat from the sun

Sunlight reflected by the surface

Sunlight absorbed at surface

Human activities release Greenhouse gases

CFCs and Haloalkane
Refrigerators
Aerosols

Nitrous oxide
Gasoline
Agriculture

Methane
Cattle
Fertilizer

Carbon dioxide
Oil
Coal

Several areas of the world have been drier and hotter than usual. Many of the recent wildfires were in areas experiencing droughts. California, Siberia, and Australia were all suffering from unusually hot temperatures. They also had very little rainfall over a long period of time. These conditions created the perfect place for fires to run wild.

Strong winds create dust storms in drought-stricken parts of Australia.

FIRE SUPPRESSION

Another factor leading to more and larger wildfires comes from years of fire suppression. Wildfires weren't allowed to burn. In the late 1800s and early 1900s, the U.S. experienced some very damaging and deadly wildfires. Because of this, policies were enacted to put out fires immediately. Fire lookout towers were built. Firefighting crews were formed to cover different forests. It worked and helped reduce the amount of land burned by wildfires each year. But it came at a price, which we are paying for today.

Fire lookout towers let people spot wildfires more quickly so they could stop them from spreading in a forest.

Wildfires are sometimes necessary. They keep ecosystems healthy. They thin out thick forests. They encourage new plant growth. Over time, forests become overgrown. Trees so close together allow fire to spread faster. Dead plants and trees also litter the forest floor. They dry up and become more fuel for a fire.

Beginning in the 1970s, policies changed. People realized wildfires were important for forests. They focused more on controlling them so they didn't get out of hand. But some forests today remain overgrown because of the earlier practices. So when a wildfire begins in one of these areas, it can quickly grow to an uncontrollable size. The site of the Dixie Fire was one of those places.

Removing dry brush helps forest workers control the spread of fires.

YELLOWSTONE FIRES

In June 1988, lightning started 18 fires in Yellowstone National Park. The fires were allowed to burn as part of the policy change the previous decade. Forest managers predicted they would be put out by the July rain. But the rain never came. The fire ended up burning nearly 800,000 acres (324,000 hectares) of the park. The rain and snow that fell on September 11 of that year helped extinguish the blaze.

It may seem impossible for firefighters to bring these massive wildfires under control. But they have different strategies they use to do just that. They remove heat and oxygen by adding water or chemicals. Ground crews spray the flames using special fire trucks or water pumps. Airplanes and helicopters fight from the sky, dropping water and chemicals over large areas. They remove fuel by clearing large areas of anything that can burn. Crews may also fight fire with fires. They start controlled fires around the wildfire. This takes away the fuel for the approaching flames.

A plane dumps water on a wildfire in Greece in 2021.

Putting out wildfires is not always easy or quick. Fires can be unpredictable. It can take months of tireless work to get these fires contained. And after the last ember finally burns out, you're left with the aftermath. Sometimes, that can be more disastrous than the fire itself.

THE HEROES

Firefighters that help prevent and battle wildfires have special skills and training. Ground crews work with fire engines and hoses. They dig trenches around the fire to help stop the spread. Smoke jumpers parachute into remote areas to fight the flames. Helitack crews hang from helicopters with chainsaws to clear trees.

FACT
In extreme fires, flames can reach more than 160 feet (49 m) high. Temperatures can be nearly 2,200 degrees Fahrenheit (1,200 degrees Celsius).

The effects from wildfires can spread far and wide. Large fires release carbon dioxide and other greenhouse gases into the air. This leads to more rapid climate change. The warming causes hotter and drier weather. It lengthens the fire season in many areas. It's a vicious cycle—climate change leads to bigger wildfires, while wildfires worsen climate change.

FLEEING THE FIRE

Wildfires also have a big effect on people. Homes in the path of the fire are reduced to ashes. Lives are interrupted, and the fires can also cause health problems. Smoke from wildfires pollutes the air. Tiny bits of ash float into the sky. Wind can blow this smoke thousands of miles away. You don't need to be near the fire to be affected by it. Inhaling this air can make breathing difficult.

Smoke fills the sky during the wildfire near Salinas, California, in 2020.

Fires force deer to escape their forest habitat.

Like people, animals must flee their homes during wildfires. Some run into populated areas. There are risks of being hit by cars or attacked by people's pets. These mass movements can also result in too many animals in one territory. There may not be enough food, water, and shelter for all of them. Sadly, not all animals make it out of wildfires. The heavy smoke can confuse them. Fires spreading in different directions can trap them.

FACT
The 2021 wildfires around the world put a record amount of carbon dioxide into the air. It was more than twice what the country of Germany emits in a whole year.

NOT OVER YET

The environment can take a huge hit from wildfires. While the fire may be out, more natural disasters can follow.

Heavy rains washing over burned ground caused mud and debris to fill a street.

If heavy rains fall soon after a wildfire, that can bring on a new set of problems. Have you ever emptied a bucket of water onto very dry ground? The water cannot easily soak in. It spreads out, covering a much larger area. Imagine a storm dropping heavy rains onto the scorched ground after a wildfire. Water piles up on top of the dry, hard ground. It can't soak in as fast as it's falling. This is how flash floods occur.

flows. Trees and plants keep soil from eroding. But after a wildfire, there is nothing left to hold the soil in place. These burned soils and ashes can be washed into rivers and streams. In large amounts, this can cause algae to grow. Algae use up the oxygen in the water, making it hard for fish and other water animals to survive.

After a wildfire, it can be hard to imagine a forest ever looking the same again. But from the ashes, new life will begin.

A landslide covered a road in the Dixie Fire area in California.

CHAPTER 5
RECOVERY AND THE FUTURE

Forests have an amazing ability to heal and regrow. The speed of regrowth depends on the severity of the wildfire. Forests can regenerate quickly after smaller wildfires. But after large wildfires, it can take decades to recover. Regrowth usually happens in stages:

1. Wildflowers and weeds are the first to emerge. They grow quickly and create new seeds.

2. Grasses begin to grow. They take over and replace a lot of the weeds.

3. Slow-growing trees like red cedar, pines, alder, and aspen begin to sprout. They are able to grow and survive in dry areas with soil that doesn't have a lot of nutrients.

4. The forest canopy begins to fill in. It provides shade for the forest floor. Needles and leaves fall to the ground. They help create new, healthy topsoil.

5. Taller trees such as maples, oaks, and hickories, grow last. They need a healthy environment to survive. When these trees appear, the forest is back to a strong state.

THE ANIMALS RETURN

Animals also return in stages after a wildfire. Insects come and eat the burned trees. These insects then attract birds and other predators. Small mammals, such as squirrels and chipmunks, soon join them. Animals that can make homes in the fallen trees, such as foxes and raccoons, are next. Once enough plants and grasses have grown, deer and other large animals move back.

The size and intensity of wildfires is growing. The fires in Australia, California, and Russia have shown the usual ways of controlling these fires are not working. Forest workers and leaders are looking for new ways to help prevent these infernos in the future.

A firefighter starts brush on fire on purpose.

One of the main reasons wildfires grow so big is because of the forest overgrowth. More prescribed burns are being planned. Prescribed burns are fires started, closely watched, and controlled by firefighters. It is a safer way to thin out a forest. Doing these prescribed burns will help to avoid such large wildfires.

In September 2021, wildfires were coming very close to Sequoia National Forest in California. It is home to some of the largest trees in the world. Prescribed fires have been done in this forest since the 1960s. The wildfires did eventually invade Sequoia National Forest. But the devastation could have been far worse if the prescribed burns hadn't been performed.

A eucalyptus tree sprouts after burning in an Australian fire.

Wildfires are a part of life. As long as there is heat, fuel, and oxygen, wildfires will occur. It's a way for nature to reset. Dead, fallen trees are replaced with strong, new saplings. A once dark and shaded forest floor comes to life with green grasses and colorful wildflowers. It can be hard to see past the destruction at first. But remember, from each wildfire comes new life.

FACT
General Sherman is in the Sequoia National Forest and is the largest tree in the world. Firefighters wrapped the base of the tree in fire-resistant material to keep it safe from the approaching wildfires.

GLOSSARY

algae (AL-jee)—small plants without roots or stems that grow in water or on damp surfaces

chemical (KE-muh-kuhl)—a substance used in or produced by chemistry

debris (duh-BREE)—loose, natural materials

debris flow (duh-BREE FLO)—fast-moving landslides carrying rocks, trees, and other large objects

ecosystem (EE-koh-sis-tuhm)—a system of living and nonliving things in an environment

evacuate (i-VA-kyuh-wayt)—to leave an area during a time of danger

greenhouse gases (GREEN-houss GA-suhs)—gases in Earth's atmosphere that trap heat energy from the sun

ignite (ig-NITE)—to set fire to something

nutrient (NOO-tree-uhnt)—a substance needed by a living thing to stay healthy

regenerate (re-JEN-uh-rayt)—to make new

suppress (SUH-press)—to prevent something from happening

terrain (tuh-RAYN)—the surface of the land

vapor (VAY-pur)—a gas made from a liquid

READ MORE

Maurer, Tracy Nelson. *The World's Worst Wildfires*. North Mankato, MN: Capstone Press, 2019.

Potenza, Alessandra. *All About Wildfires*. New York: Children's Press, 2021.

Williams, Olivia. *Understanding Wildfires*. Ann Arbor, MI: Cherry Lake Press, 2022.

INTERNET SITES

Smokey for Kids
smokeybear.com/en/smokey-for-kids

Wildfires
ready.gov/kids/disaster-facts/wildfires

Wildfires—How They Spread
easyscienceforkids.com/all-about-wildfires/

INDEX

ABOUT THE AUTHOR

Jaclyn Jaycox is an editor and author of more than 80 children's books. Natural disasters and extreme weather are among her favorite topics to write about. They have interested her since childhood, always curious and in awe over what Mother Nature is capable of. She'd watch excitedly as big storms rolled in, until her parents would pull her away from the window to somewhere safe. While writing *Wildfire, Inside the Inferno*, Jaclyn spent hours reading news articles and watching footage of recent fires with that same curiosity and awe. Jaclyn lives in Minnesota with her husband and two children.